THE WORLD ACCORDING TO
DINOSAURS

Belle Hansen
and Amelia Newman

CURRENCY PRESS
The performing arts publisher

CURRENT THEATRE SERIES

First published in 2023
by Currency Press Pty Ltd,
PO Box 2287, Strawberry Hills, NSW, 2012, Australia
enquiries@currency.com.au
www.currency.com.au

in association with La Mama

Copyright: *The World According to Dinosaurs* © Belle Hansen and Amelia Newman, 2023.

COPYING FOR EDUCATIONAL PURPOSES
The Australian *Copyright Act 1968* [Act] allows a maximum of one chapter or 10% of this book, whichever is the greater, to be copied by any educational institution for its educational purposes provided that that educational institution [or the body that administers it] has given a remuneration notice to Copyright Agency [CA] under the Act.
For details of the CA licence for educational institutions contact CA, 12/66 Goulburn Street, Sydney, NSW, 2000; tel: within Australia 1800 066 844 toll free; outside Australia 61 2 9394 7600; fax: 61 2 9394 7601; email: memberservices@copyright.com.au

COPYING FOR OTHER PURPOSES
Except as permitted under the Act, for example a fair dealing for the purposes of study, research, criticism or review, no part of this book may be reproduced, stored in a retrieval system, or transmitted in any form or by any means without prior written permission. All enquiries should be made to the publisher at the address above.

Any performance or public reading of *The World According to Dinosaurs* is forbidden unless a licence has been received from the author or the author's agent. The purchase of this book in no way gives the purchaser the right to perform the play in public, whether by means of a staged production or a reading. All applications for public performance should be addressed to the authors c/- Currency Press at the address above.

Typeset by Brighton Gray for Currency Press.
Cover features Belle Hansen and Amelia Newman; image by Darren Gill.
Cover design by Mathias Johansson.

Currency Press acknowledges the Traditional Owners of the Country on which we live and work. We pay our respects to all Aboriginal and Torres Strait Islander Elders, past and present.

A catalogue record for this book is available from the National Library of Australia

Contents

THE WORLD ACCORDING TO DINOSAURS 1

Theatre Program at the end of the playtext

This script was written and developed on the land of the Wurundjeri people of the Kulin Nation. The project was developed and rehearsed on the land of Wadawurrung people. When the script is performed please acknowledge where it was written, in addition to the land it is currently being performed on.

The World According to Dinosaurs was first produced by Frenzy Theatre Co and La Mama at Platform Arts, Geelong, on 4 May 2023, with the following cast:

A	Amelia Newman
B	Belle Hansen
ENSEMBLE	Izzy Patane,
	Matilda Gibbs,
	Anna Louey,
	Chris Patrick Hansen,
	Michael Cooper,
	Emily Pearson

Director, Cassandra Gray
Producer, Flick
Sound Designer and Composer, Jack Burmeister
Lighting Designer, Theo Viney
Education Manager, Alex Veljanovksi
Stage Manager, Brigitte Jennings

CHARACTERS

A, cheerful, easily distracted.

B, hard worker, focused.

ENSEMBLE, playing various characters, including Gary from Coburg North, Little Betty, etc.

NOTE

All characters can be played by anyone of any gender. Performers and makers are encouraged to change language to suit their team, e.g. Little Betty can become Little Bobby.

The ensemble is flexible depending on your production requirements and can be cut to support scene study work or expanded for accessibility.

SETTING

Busy café. The world is ending.

This show is made for maximalism.

GENRE

Genres change throughout the work, using what is stated in the text as a jumping-off point. Physical theatre conventions are the grounding genre of the overall work.

This play text went to press before the end of rehearsals and may differ from the play as performed.

OPENING

The stage is in darkness.

VOICEOVER: This is a story. A story told today: about a tomorrow for us, but a yesterday for them. A recollection of memories and events that occurred when the world as we knew it ended. Two people, of usually little importance, became the two most important people in the world. Though we are unable to definitively say that this is how the events occurred on this day, there have been many findings that suggest they did. This is the end of the world. The World According to—

Lights flash up and the café is in full swing.

B is on the coffee machine and A is outside collecting dishes.

CUSTOMERS *are already waiting and others appear over this section.*

A: Hey you! Good to see you
ENSEMBLE MEMBER: Hi!

A puts the dishes to the side. B side-eyes the pile.

A: Just the usual today? Strong capp and soy latte?
ENSEMBLE MEMBER: Yes please
A: Lovely! Twelve dollars fifty. Just tap when you are ready

ENSEMBLE MEMBER beeps their card. Another person appears.

Alrighty who was next? Oh hey mate, how are you going today?
ENSEMBLE MEMBER: Not bad, not bad at all!
A: You seemed chuffed, I assume the presentation thing went well?
ENSEMBLE MEMBER: Oh yeah it was great! Very happy with how it went!
A: Oh my goodness, so remind me ...
ENSEMBLE MEMBER: A piccolo and two / extra-hot capps
A: Extra-hot capps! Beautiful.
ENSEMBLE MEMBER: Can you please remind the barista to make it extra-hot? They were a bit lukewarm last time.
A: Did you get that?
B: Yep.

ENSEMBLE MEMBER: Extra-hot!
A: Gotcha

Strong weather occurs.

A: Crazy weather today. Here are your coffees
ENSEMBLE MEMBER: Crazy weather today! Thanks so much!
B: Can you send these out to table three?
A: Sure thing

A *carries out a tray of coffees—*

VOICEOVER: Now left alone, our intrepid hero can finally get some work done. Even in the face of extreme weather conditions, this barista will continue to create latte art.

Weather stops.

B: [*to customer*] Hi
ENSEMBLE MEMBER: Two lattes

B *makes coffees at a unrealistic speed.*

B: Here you go ... Hello
ENSEMBLE MEMBER: Large cappuccino please.
B: Enjoy. Next.
ENSEMBLE MEMBER: Weak mocha.
B: Weak chocolate or weak coffee.
ENSEMBLE MEMBER: Weak coffee
B: Okay. Here you go.

Something pings on B's phone—they start on a takeaway order.

VOICEOVER: Ah a classic call to action! Text message from the pharmacy across the road asking for their regular order.

A *walks back in—the customers light up when they interact with* A.

All heroes must have a foil, a traditional buffoon sidekick to demonstrate the hero's practicality and greatness.

A: Bye! Enjoy! Have a good day!

A *puts the dirty dishes in the sink—the busyness dissipates.*

[*to* B] Do you know what dialectics is?

VOICEOVER: Our hero has an extensive knowledge of Hegel's dialectic method

B: Yes. Take these across to the pharmacy.

    B *hands* A *a tray of coffees.*

A: Okay!

    B *hears a low rumble sound move across the stage.*

    A *returns.*

A: Hey! I saw a chicken.

B: Okay … what?

A: I saw a chicken … I saw a chicken! There was a chicken outside walking and a person was following it.

    B *looks outside.*

B: So there is … what a calm bird.

    They continue watching the chicken.

A: You know how dinosaurs are most closely related to birds?

B: To birds?

A: Well, well, well scientists, what they did was, they stuck a pole-like thing on a chicken's butt to simulate a T-Rex's tail and the chicken bent over really low to balance—

B: Hmm balance

A: Which led them to consider that T-Rex was actually bent over, like really low, and didn't stand upright. The big tail was actually to counterweight the T-Rex's huge head—

B: [*sarcastically*] Oh no, not the head.

A: And that chickens actually have really similar neck muscles to T-Rexes, they have found from muscle reconstruction of fossil records—

    B *notices chicken walker looking at them.*

VOICEOVER: See our hero here did not know their counterpart had such extensive knowledge in the sciences, they always assumed their interests did not extend past their own nose

A: Which explains why T-Rex's hands were so small! They were actually close to the ground like juvenile arms, T-Rex grew up but the arms stayed low. Imagine a grown man with a boy's arms.

B: Can you take the rubbish?

PUMPKIN

A pregnant ENSEMBLE MEMBER *comes in and is looking at the counter.*

A: Hello, can I help you with anything today?

ENSEMBLE MEMBER: Oh hello, um yes, I'm just looking, I'm not sure ... this pumpkin thing, the focaccia, does it have unpasteurised cheese in it?

A: Oh the focaccia. It's like hard cheese, but it has probably touched some soft cheeses in its ... umm life ...

ENSEMBLE MEMBER: Ahhh yeah hmm

A: Hmm yeah, I can put it in the oven and blast it with high heat?

ENSEMBLE MEMBER: That would be so helpful. Thank you so much!

A: No worries

    A *leaves with the pumpkin focaccia.*

ENSEMBLE MEMBER: [*to* B] Thanks again

B: It's fine.

ENSEMBLE MEMBER: It's just so hard to know what's okay to eat when you're pregnant

B: Mmm ... pregnant ...

ENSEMBLE MEMBER: Yeah, thanks again, I don't mean to be a pain

B: No, no

ENSEMBLE MEMBER: Oh no I must be the worst!

B: There was a regular just this morning who called me a— [*Long beeped-out slur*] —when the price of their almond capp went up by fifty cents. I said 'What do you want me to do ... ?! The supplier has a shortage of coffee beans because of last year's hurricanes that ripped through the coffee belt destroying a lot of the independent farms that the coffee industry thrives on, or exploits.'

ENSEMBLE MEMBER: Oh ... may I have decaf?

B: Yes, of course. I said to them, 'I *can* take off the fifty-cent addition today, because you didn't know, but I don't want you telling another barista that last time you got a discount and that they should honour that too. Honestly that isn't worth my time, to have this conversation with you now because you can't fork out another fifty cents *today* and then get pulled up on it *tomorrow* because I was just trying to be kind once and you don't understand the difference between a one-off kindness and the consistent special treatment that you are clearly craving.' They were probably the worst ... today.

Awkward pause.

A: Your focaccia!
B: Your coffee.
ENSEMBLE MEMBER: [*uncomfortably*] Thank you both.

Pregnant customer leaves.

B: So irresponsible
A: Why? It's human instinct.
B: You'd bring a child into this mess—
A: We're all animals, it's our purpose to keep on keeping on until the asteroid.
B: There is no asteroid, it's not going to be that easy.
A: You think the asteroid was easy? It wasn't a quickie—
B: A quickie?
A: Ya know, quick bang and explosive finish.
B: That's disgusting.
A: The dinosaurs took millions of years to become extinct after that event.
B: I'm sure it wasn't a pleasant few million years—
A: Twenty-five percent of them survived it too—
B: Why does that even matter?
A: Maybe it means that we have a chance?
B: I don't know how you're confusing slowly suffocating on a cloud of ash and a chance.
VOICEOVER: Conflict is the only thing that can drive narrative forward. Two individuals with differences in perspective creates friction. But wait, this is only page five? Isn't this a little early?
A: I don't want to sound all ... I dunno ... but like, we are only basing the end of the world off humanity's knowledge. As a species we have been wrong more times than we've been right.
B: I hope you're having fun on that limb out there by yourself. Tell me what your friends the dinosaurs think.
A: We can't ask another species what they think, there is not an inter-species summit, and that's our own fault, humanity's fault.
B: Quick grab the phone and I'll call the eagles, get them to weigh in— they probably have a better vantage point from the sky.

A: I know you're mocking me but—
B: Here we go—
A: Don't dismiss me!
B: Next you're going to tell me if we all went vegan and substituted meat for pumpkins we would not be in this mess.
A: That's not what I'm saying
B: I hate pumpkin!
A: Then eat eggplant. What were we talking about?
VOICEOVER: But sometimes you just want your co-worker to shut up. I suppose it's an intention.
B: You were about to / take the rubbish

> *Four sock puppets of dinosaurs pop up from behind the counter over this section. Very demonstrative and childlike. Space for additional ensemble choreography.*
>
> *A* Play School-*like theme song starts to play in the background.*

A: Oh yeah! Okay, here is the thing that gets me about the dinosaurs' representation in the media. Dinosaurs are all grey and green in the movies, which is crazy, because you think of their relatives, descendants and look at birds as a connection to the non-avian dinosaurs. The large ones, they were screwed by the extinction event. It's their small relatives that would have been able to survive. They're now chickens, cassowaries, turkeys, like … they all have dark colour palettes and then pops of blue and red. It wouldn't be wrong to consider that larger dinosaurs had a similar colour palette. This idea that they were all grey and green comes from the crocodilians because they are living dinosaurs that survive in water and need that camo for their environment. But, the T-Rex? Did T-Rex need to blend into water or did T-Rex need to look menacing and shocking! Like a cassowary perhaps?! Anyway I like to imagine that T-Rex had a bright blue nose and was black all over, red all over! Chickens are orange! They are orange!

> *The two* ENSEMBLE MEMBERS *stand up in puppetry blacks and stare at the audience while they take off the sock puppets.*

B: The rubbish.
A: What? Oh yeah sorry

> B *is trying to clean as quickly as possible while* A *walks away.*

A: Wait …
B: Oh my god.
A: So they took a 3D scan of T-Rex's skull and found out what T-Rex's inner ear looks like
B: Okay.
A: And like, what an animal is good at hearing is an indication of what the animal could have sounded like
B: That doesn't make sense, I can hear everything but I can't make every sound.
A: That's not how it works and you definitely cannot hear everything.
B: I wish I couldn't hear you
A: Just listen, it's good, I promise!
B: …
A: So, T-Rex could hear low frequencies, so low that when scientists tried to recreate it, they had to use a mixture of whale song and bird noises and it was almost too low for the human ear
B: Spooky.
A: Yeah!
B: Bins … Please …

> A *finally exits with the bins.*
>
> B *cleans. They hear the T-Rex sounds again. But they know what it is now. Louder this time.*

THE AWKWARD INTERACTION

A customer enters—they recognise B *from a one-night stand.*

A song like 'Wicked Game' by Chris Isaak starts playing and a disco ball rotates above their heads. They awkwardly dance together like it's a prom.

ENSEMBLE MEMBER: Oh hi!
B: Oh. Hi.
ENSEMBLE MEMBER: I didn't know you worked here
B: Yeah … It's temporary
ENSEMBLE MEMBER: Cos weren't you studying … something?

B: Yeah, yeah, something … Haha
ENSEMBLE MEMBER: Oh haha
VOICEOVER: The genre indicates that these two are supposed to get together but I have a feeling that isn't how this is going to go.
ENSEMBLE MEMBER: Did you miss me?
B: I barely know you …
ENSEMBLE MEMBER: You can miss someone you barely know
B: That doesn't sound like me, I don't really miss people.
ENSEMBLE MEMBER: That's something 'someone who misses people' would say.
B: I wouldn't do that to myself
ENSEMBLE MEMBER: You can't control something like that—
B: Can't I? I've been pretty successful so far—I haven't cried or broken down or taken a day off or run away yet. Maybe I'm just stronger than everyone else.
ENSEMBLE MEMBER: It's going to hurt so much more if you don't start to process it soon.

Hard cut and return to the café world. Some remnants of the prom are still present, like the disco ball is still lowered, but the lights are back to café lights.

B: Do you want something?
ENSEMBLE MEMBER: Pardon me?
B: From the café? I can make a coffee?
ENSEMBLE MEMBER: Oh yes! I forget where I am and I just saw you and I …
B: Okay
ENSEMBLE MEMBER: Strong flat white please … with, um, soy milk
B: Cool.

B *turns away to make the coffee.*

A *re-enters. They aren't wearing shoes or their appearance is altered in a strange way. They pick up the weird vibe from* B *and* ENSEMBLE MEMBER.

A: Hi, have you ordered?
ENSEMBLE MEMBER: Yeah, yeah
A: Okay, that will be five dollars

B: Soy
A: Oh five fifty with soy thanks

Long awkward pause while coffee is made.

ENSEMBLE MEMBER: I got a lizard.
A: What's its name?
ENSEMBLE MEMBER: Shrek
B: Your coffee ... Bye!
ENSEMBLE MEMBER: ... Goodbye

ENSEMBLE MEMBER *leaves the café.*

A: Was that a friend?
B: I just know them
A: There was just like a tension, I was like what's going on? Did someone fart or do the hanky panky or—
B: Do I seem like someone who would hook up with random people?
A: No?
B: Because I'm not—
A: Okay, well they seemed nice
B: And their house smelt like rabbits and heat lamps.

A *is confused by this.*

Can you release the pressure in the steam wand?
A: The steam wand ... yeah cool ... I could do that ...
B: But?
A: You'd have to show me how to again first.
B: We literally just did this yesterday—
A: I know, I know—I just don't care about my job, have no work ethic and want to make everything harder for you.
VOICEOVER: That comment may not be historically accurate.
B: I appreciate you coming in every day, your smile is infectious and you make my world a whole lot brighter.
VOICEOVER: That doesn't sound quite right either.
A: Let's go over it one more time and do it with a little pizazz!

THE LATE LATE UNDER-RESEARCHED TALK SHOW

VOICEOVER: Now from a little café in a suburb just like any other we have …

Drum roll.

B: Me!! And I am going to show you the correct way to depressurise a coffee machine for a healthy planet

ENSEMBLE MEMBER: I love the planet

B: So do I! But not out of choice, out the existential awareness that we exist on one. And that awareness has driven our species insane!

B takes apart the coffee machine to reveal broken wires and mushrooms growing out of it—futuristic and organic. It starts to quietly hum like a synth. B shows this to A in an effort to show them how to depressurise the machine but A quickly gets sucked into the show.

ENSEMBLE MEMBER: What an amazing product!

VOICEOVER: Now we have our local history buff—to lecture us incessantly about what they read online at three a.m. last night, but have done no further research on! Please welcome Guy Kidson or more commonly known as GuyzWorldTheory-Two-Eight-Six-One, that's with a Z folks!

ENSEMBLE MEMBER: [*as* GUY KIDSON] Hello! YES.

Over this section the ENSEMBLE *acts as game-show assistants. The* ENSEMBLE *creates images that grow in ambition. It quickly escalates into a circus performance, a wrestling match, another visually interesting event that is somewhat connected to the topic.*

Today we are going to talk about the debate of Linguistic Relativity versus Linguistic Determinism. All hinging on the colour blue! I joined this cutting-edge new group on Facebook, which is growing exponentially, called 'What even is colour?' And it has made me literally see the whole world in a new way … or rather NOT SEE! In the history of language—

VOICEOVER: I'm just going to mute our story for a moment. This deconstruction of colour goes on for another fourteen minutes. During this time Guy Kidson will cite the following sources as professionals in this area: Reddit user AnonyMoose-Forty-Five, the song 'Mr. Blue Sky' by Electric Light Orchestra, the phrase 'Paint the town red' and the bird that flies over the rainbow in the *Wizard of Oz*. The flair and circumstance really compensates for the flimsy but impassioned research. Our valiant host struggles with editing and lacks the skills required for robust fact-checking. Maybe they need an editor, someone to bounce ideas off and cement the vision. Maybe that can be our job? Let's fast-forward?

ENSEMBLE MEMBER: [*as* GUY KIDSON] —to paraphrase a YouTube video I watched by ADAPTscience, there is an idea that if there is no word to identify the colour then the feedback loop cannot be formed in the human brain! The forty-three-minute deep-dive took us across the globe, across time and cross-referenced the entire history of mankind ... in relation to the colour, or not-colour—blue. For example *The Iliad*. Homer described the ocean as wine-dark. Perhaps Ancient Greeks couldn't even see the colour blue!

> *Cue from* VOICEOVER *to last line. The dialogue speeds up (fast-forward style) while the* ENSEMBLE *tries to keep up with the images.*

You know they have great quality control if they are posting EVERY Tuesday and Thursday! But then, strap in—GAME-CHANGER—I read a YouTube comment left by HBE-Jin-Six-Five-Seven, stating 'as someone who has studied linguistics'—which I confirmed on their instagram bio—'linguistic determinism has been disproven in the field'. And 'linguistic relativity explains that the colour is still identifiable to the human brain, it just takes longer to articulate the differences. Teal can be described as more green or more blue, by different individuals.' They said 'I also love how everyone is suddenly horned up for linguistics.' Yeah horned up indeed!

VOICEOVER: Let's stop there. This is a train of thought that could run itself into the ground. Amazing how the mind can sustain itself.

> *The* ENSEMBLE *stops and kidnaps a fellow* ENSEMBLE MEMBER, *dragging them off the stage screaming behind a covered mouth. Everything grinds to a halt.* B *is tired.*
>
> *A customer enters and the game show stops. Record scratch.*

B: We are closed.

ENSEMBLE MEMBER: Oh … I just wanted a coffee

Sounds of screaming continue.

A: Sorry, we have already cleaned the machine.

The customer leaves disgruntled.

B: The sign says we are closed
A: Can't people read?
B: So rude
A: What a moron, honestly …
B: Totally
A: Okay, you keep going on the machine, I will pack this up.
B: No, I just showed you how to do it.
A: But I got distracted by Guy's World Theory!
B: Figure it out, I'm not showing you again.
A: I do work! You just don't see me work!
B: Likely story.

CAFÉ RESET: CLEAN AS YOU GO

VOICEOVER: There comes a time where our heroes must toil relentlessly thus earning their triumphant climatic moment at the end of the story
B: Have you finished the weekly wipey-cleany list?
A: Yep
B: Ice sink?
A: Yep
B: Cleaned the coffee machine?
A: Yep
B: Taken it out / to the dishwasher, yep.
A: —to the dishwasher, yep.
VOICEOVER: It is a truth of human nature that when two individuals are within close proximity to one another, they will eventually find common ground.
A: Filled the salt and pepper shakers?
B: Yep
A: Sugar packets?
B: Yep

VOICEOVER: Shorthand develops as individuals learn each other's patterns of behaviour.
A: Napkins?
B: Yep, ketchup?
A: Yep, toppings?
B: Yep
A: Canisters?

> B *picks up a dinosaur sock puppet.*

A: I think that's everything.

> *Pause.*

B: Spoons?
A: I haven't done the spoons.
B: I have.
A: But you just asked?
B: You said that was everything.

> *Pause.*

A: If you were a dog you would be a bull terrier!
B: You don't know me.
A: How bull terrier of you …
B: Did you actually clean the ice sink?
A: No … I totally just splashed water in it.
VOICEOVER: While our hero resents their co-worker's cavalier attitude, they admire their honesty.
B: And the steam wand pressure?
A: Yes, I am doing it right now!

RADIO GURU

A *begins to look at the steam wand, intending to release the pressure. They notice a coffee cup on a table and get distracted.* A *walks over to pick up the coffee, knocking it off the table by accident. Blue liquid pours out of the coffee cup and onto the floor.* A *spends this scene slowly cleaning up the blue liquid.*

Radio static churns in the background. An ENSEMBLE MEMBER *comes on with a 1950s-style microphone.*

A duo/trio of singers perform this song on the mic as if in an old radio booth.

Song: 'My Body is a Time Capsule':

> What will find me once I am gone?
> Will I fossilise?
> Is my future encased in stone—
> Or will worms eat my thighs?
>
> Will the world remember me?
> Where does my chapter close?
> Is it when the memory fades—
> Or when I decompose?
>
> If I'm the last one on this earth
> At least last of my kind
> How will I be studied
> If no-one is left behind.
>
> This cannot all end in nothingness
> If so that just seems cruel
> Why would I keep up the pretence
> To be shown ultimately as a fool?

At the conclusion of the song, another ENSEMBLE MEMBER *steps up as a Radio Announcer.*

ENSEMBLE MEMBER: [*as Radio Announcer*] Up next we have a call coming through on our CORNY LONG-WINDED NAME FOR A REQUEST LINE … Gary from Coburg North you're on the line.

ENSEMBLE MEMBER: [*as Gary*] You're all idiots, morons, slaves to the system. The world isn't ending, they just want you to panic and spend all your money to save their capitalist asses. Then they will come in and offer you a tiny amount of hope and you will love them because you will think they saved you. They aren't going to save you, there is nothing to be saved from. The end of the world is not near, it only feels that way because you're all blinded by fight-or-flight—

> *The radio frequency is hacked and Little Betty's voice comes through.*

ENSEMBLE MEMBER: [*as Little Betty*] Have you been in the aftermath of a real crisis? Realised you are still alive and have to decide what to do next? What you have to face next? Aftermath is a thin sharp blade. It's the end of days friends and God is here to help us

Little Betty gets cut off by Radio Announcer.

ENSEMBLE MEMBER: [*as Radio Announcer*] Sorry about that folks!

A *has finished mopping up but is dizzy. They walk slowly back towards the coffee machine and just stand there staring at the steam wand.*

WHO AM I?

B *walks back in, carrying a lot of stock.*

B: It's very slow for this time of day
A: People dropping their routines I guess
B: Their routines maybe, but coffee? I doubt it!
A: Do you wanna play Who Am I?
B: Who Am I?
A: Yeah, Who Am I?
B: Ah, how do you play?
A: You've never played?
B: I don't think so …
A: It's like one person is someone and the other asks yes or no questions …
B: Oh! Like Twenty Questions!
A: Yes! Yes! Exactly like Twenty Questions
B: I've never heard it called Who Am I?
A: We always called it that, in my house, because we never kept it to just twenty questions
B: Oh I see
A: Yeah! Okay I got someone …
B: Okay
A: Okay … ask me a question
B: Oh right … ummmmmm … hmmm is it a human?
A: Yes
B: Are they alive?
A: No.

B: Oh … are they from the 1950s?
A: Um, yes I think so
B: Frank Sinatra!
A: Oh no they were born in the early fifties maybe … wait …
VOICEOVER: If it's who you are thinking of, they were born in 1947.
A: I feel like they were born in 1947!
B: So they aren't from the fifties?
A: Well they were there
B: No I mean their era wasn't iconically the fifties.
A: Oh. No!
B: Sixties?
A: No?
B: Seventies?
A: Yeah but also …
B: Also eighties and nineties gotcha gotcha, so are they actors?
A: No, but they have been in movies
B: Okay. Okay. Sports player?
A: Heck no
B: A musician?
A: Yes!
B: Hmm Freddy Mercury
A: No but close!
VOICEOVER: Hmm I wonder if it's David Bowie
B: Um I don't know any other members of Queen
A: No, who knows any other members of Queen? He did a song with Freddie
B: He did a song with Freddie Mercury … hmm I don't know … just tell me? Is it really iconic?
VOICEOVER: It's definitely David Bowie
A: It's really iconic. You are going to be so mad when you don't get it
B: Just tell me.
A: David Bowie!
B: Oh yeah, I could see the lightning bolt
VOICEOVER: See! I knew it!
A: Yeah! I thought that would be an easy one.
B: It would be, but I kept thinking of Adam Lambert, I thought he isn't that old.

A: Oh my god
B: Okay, my turn
A: Are you alive?
B: Yes
A: Are you dead?
B: No?
A: Are you real?
B: Yes ...
A: So you aren't like a fictional character?
B: What? You're alive if you are fictional
A: Are you real if you are a fictional character or are you not alive?
B: Wait
VOICEOVER: Our heroes seemed to have abandoned their post.
A: I think you are not alive or dead. But you are real if you are fictional.

> CUSTOMERS *begin to trickle in over the next section of text. A and B are not focusing on the customers, they are consumed with their conversation.*
>
> *The* VOICEOVER *begins to serve the customers. They can hear them but A and B cannot.*

B: If you are fictional you are alive, unless you die in the story.
A: But Harry Potter isn't an alive person
B: He is alive in the story and Dumbledore is famously dead so Dumbledore would be a dead fictional person
VOICEOVER: [*to customer*] I think you'll just have to make it yourself.

> *The customers make their own coffee.*

A: Oh my god, so true
B: Wait I've confused myself, I'm starting over
A: Okay, are you alive?
B: Yes
A: Are you an actor?
B: Yes
VOICEOVER: Five dollars, tap when you're ready.
ENSEMBLE MEMBER: It has almond milk.
VOICEOVER: Oh right, seven dollars and eighty cents. Camel-milk cappuccino? Five dollars and twenty cents. Two goat-milk lattes?

Eight dollars and eighty cents. How many espressos? Five? Okay, Twenty-four dollars and ninety cents. A cow's-milk latte? That will be nine dollars. They have other options? Okay … Tap please. Soy-milk mocha?

> *The customer pays for the coffee they made themselves and then sits down. Other* CUSTOMERS *who have entered witness the interaction and do similar things to get their food and coffee.*

A: Are you British?
B: Yes
A: Benedict Cumberbatch?
B: No
A: Oh Kate Winslet!
B: Yes! Love her
A: She was mesmerising in *Eternal Sunshine of the Spotless Mind* … OH and she plays a palaeontologist in *Ammonite*!!
B: *The Holiday* with Cameron Diaz is fucking iconic—
A: *Sense and Sensibility*
B: and *Divergent*
A: *The Dressmaker*
B: *Insurgent*
A: *Enigma*
B: *Flushed Away*
A: *Contagion*
B: Wait …That is not a good movie—
A: what *Divergent*, *Insurgent* and *Flushed Away* are?
B: Do NOT come for *Flushed Away*! Those little rats have hearts!
A: Her characters don't seem to take to water very well …
B: Yeah *Flushed Away* and *Titanic* …

> A *laughs.*

I've always wanted someone to make a horror indie film about the bodies left on the ocean floor
A: That's horrific—
B: —and yet so intriguing right?!

DANCE OF THE SINKING BODIES

B: Sinking and spiralling between suspended convulsions, your nerves like needles. A vortex of suction pulls you down quickly, silently, as the air in the ship is displaced and fights its way back to the surface. Your insides are tampered by the building pressure, cracking, popping, tearing, broken. Then you'd hit the bottom of the bathypelagic ocean layer. Darkness. The creatures down here don't have eyes. They move slowly, their skin is soft and their bodies slimy—they don't get a feast like this often. The amphipods sense your presence, a calling card of protein and fatty acids—they land gently upon your corpse and begin masticating on your outer layer: hair follicles, tooth enamel, the depths of your cuticles. As they burrow deeper through your skin and veins your scent begins to radiate across the ocean floor. The scavenger animals are waiting. They follow the trail in a frenzy, viciously searching for its source. They come in the thousands and devour the creatures buried deep within your carcass before the sand even settles behind them. Whales are skeletonised on the deep-sea floor in less than five days.

A: So how quickly would we disappear in comparison?

B: Five-point-zero-six minutes.

A: God

B: Yep

A: Chilling

B: Chilled

A: Are we considered a protein or a fatty acid?

B: I dunno, it wasn't on the Wiki page.

A: You got all of this from Wikipedia?

B: Yeah I was hyperlink-jumping—

A: As you do—

B: Of course, and I also found these things called zombie worms

A: Cool BRAINS

B: More like BONES—They sit in the rotting bones of the massive whale carcass and slowly consume them from the inside out and they do it all without a mouth. They eat through their skin and the male worms live inside the female worms, hundreds at a time. She has a colony of men being fed like children in a womb.

A: Typical

B: What?

A: Men feeding off women's success.

B: Indeed

A: I am so grateful I am not living on an ocean colony

B: Not so fast—they have a good old cousin on the land too—

A: Fuck, no

B: The land one kills insects and controls them like a puppet master from the inside for days until they are eaten by a bird, and lay their eggs inside its stomach to reproduce through its faeces.

A: It's the Trojan horse of worms?

B: Wears its victims like a suit of armour

Pause.

A: I've always been worried I'd get a tapeworm and have to do that pencil-winding thing …

B: Tapeworms are a myth

A: Huh?

B: Yep saw it on Reddit—

A: But ummm—

B: Have you ever seen a tapeworm?

A: No but—

CUSTOMER *enters.*

B: Hi what can I get ya?

Gives A *a subtle cheeky rude finger.*

ENSEMBLE MEMBER: Hi, sorry to interrupt

B: That's okay! I was done with this one anyway! [*To* A] Jump on the machine please

A: Okedoke

ENSEMBLE MEMBER: Cappuccino with cashew milk. Please.

The coffee machine spits at A.

COFFEE MACHINE BREAKDOWN

Otherworldly coffee machine breaking-down sounds underpin this whole scene. The ENSEMBLE *becomes members of the sci-fi world.*

A: Why is it doing that?
B: It's because you didn't clean it properly.
A: But I cleaned the coffee grinder?
VOICEOVER: A crew is only as capable as its ship.
B: No, I'm talking about the steam wand
A: I thought I did …
B: It doesn't make these noises when it's clean
A: It sounds broken
B: It's not. It just needs the pressure released
VOICEOVER: It takes quick thinking of a star-ship captain to regain control of its ship.
A: Do we get a new one?
B: No point
A: Can you do it?
B: I'm not doing your job for you anymore
A: Oh, I didn't mean—
B: Can you froth the milk?
A: What kind of milk?
B: Cappuccino on cashew milk
A: [*quietly to self, frustrated*] Cashew capp, cashew capp, cashew capp.

    A *strange blue liquid starts to seep out of* A*'s ear.*

B: What is your problem?
A: The steam … filter … drip, cup, bean —
B: The wand.
A: Yes, that!

    Sound stops, B *stares at* A.

B: It's done

    A *hands coffee to customer.*

    Customer exists.

B: God you're a sook.
A: That seriously can't be the—
VOICEOVER: The grind of capitalism can erode on weary individuals. But strength comes from within. Especially in the face of brewing disaster.
B: [*to a new customer*] Hi, what can I get you?
ENSEMBLE MEMBER: A shot of coffee with a large cup of almond-milk foam please!
B: [*to* A] A shot of coffee with a large cup of almond-milk foam please!

> A *makes coffee very quickly.*

ENSEMBLE MEMBER: Is this a large?
A: Yep
ENSEMBLE MEMBER: It is not very large.
A: It's not the largest kind of large, but it's pretty big—
ENSEMBLE MEMBER: You call this big?
A: I call it large
ENSEMBLE MEMBER: Your shots are all off, this is blatant disproportionate sizing.

> A *and* B *look at each other with the look of 'We just work here. Do you really think we control the sizing?' They decide to snap back.*

A: What does blatant disproportionate sizing mean? Do you know what that means?
B: I just work at a café, how would I know?
A: Well I only just learnt how to clean the machine yesterday.
B: Although, I used to work for a research organisation that ran the census, when that was still a thing. There were issues with disproportionate sizing of sample groups. The socio-economic standing of the sample groups usually held a certain level of privilege, for example they had access to phones, the internet, spoke English fluently, were able to purchase their daily almond-foam coffee.
A: Wow, you're so smart!
B: I have a postgraduate degree in social sciences with a minor in economics. But I suppose with only a minor I must have no idea what I am talking about.
A: Whereas, I'm just thinking about snacks honestly. Like the back of the box says I should only have two Oreos but I always eat at least four. Is that disproportionate sizing?

ENSEMBLE MEMBER: I just want a coffee
A: Yes. One LARGE coffee
B: Don't let it get cold.

> A *and* B *hold their contempt as the coffee machine sound morphs into the rumbling sound of a T-Rex. It is low and atmospheric and moves us into the next sequence.*

A: Do you have Wi-Fi?
B: Ugh. We've lost the internet. Where's the radio?

> *Static, sounds of chaos, real news reports from throughout history.*

THE NEWS

A and B listen to the radio and carry on with work.

ENSEMBLE MEMBER 1: The disaster in the rural community is truly devastating. The sinkhole has left many homes and buildings destroyed, and emergency responders are working tirelessly to rescue those who are still trapped. It's clear that the town's infrastructure wasn't designed to handle the high levels of population growth that have occurred in recent years.

> ENSEMBLE MEMBER 2 *joins in.*

ENSEMBLE MEMBER 1/ENSEMBLE MEMBER 2: In other news, the discovery of the sunken *Titanic* continues to fascinate researchers and historians. The wreckage and the bodies of passengers and crew members still lie on the ocean floor, serving as a reminder of the tragic events that occurred over a century ago.

ENSEMBLE MEMBER 2: It's a tragic situation indeed. And it's not just in rural communities. Overpopulation has led to an increase in paved surfaces and other impervious surfaces, which makes it difficult for water to infiltrate the ground. When heavy rains occur, the excess water flows into streams and rivers, causing devastating floods. In fact, some areas that have been hit by natural disasters have seen people resort to cannibalism just to survive.

> ENSEMBLE MEMBER 3 *joins in.*

ENSEMBLE MEMBER 2/ENSEMBLE MEMBER 3: And in the coffee belt, the region is experiencing an increase in hurricane activity, which is impacting the growth and production of coffee beans. This could have a significant impact on the coffee industry and the livelihoods of those who depend on it.

ENSEMBLE MEMBER 3: Yes, that's right. In one area, a powerful earthquake struck a remote village, leaving behind a trail of destruction and claiming countless lives. With no access to food, water, or medical aid, the survivors were forced to scavenge for whatever they could find. As the days turned into weeks and supplies ran out, some villagers reportedly began to turn on each other, resorting to cannibalism to stay alive.

ENSEMBLE MEMBER 4 *joins in.*

ENSEMBLE MEMBER 3/ENSEMBLE MEMBER 4: On a lighter note, have you ever heard of cassowaries? These large, flightless birds are known for their striking appearance and vibrant blue necks. They can be found in the rainforests of Australia and New Guinea.

ENSEMBLE MEMBER 4: Wow, that's truly horrifying. And it's not just natural disasters that can lead to desperate acts like cannibalism. There have been reports of individuals turning into fossil-like statues, possibly due to an impending ice age. The potential consequences of an ice age could be catastrophic, with the extinction of numerous species, including humans.

Speaking of vibrant colours, it's almost pumpkin season, and people are already decorating their homes with pumpkins of all shapes and sizes. From pumpkin pies to pumpkin-spice lattes, this versatile fruit has become a staple of fall cuisine.

ENSEMBLE MEMBER 1: Wait, turning into fossil-like statues? That sounds like something out of a science-fiction movie.

ENSEMBLE MEMBER 2: It's not entirely clear what's causing it, but some experts believe that it could be a side effect of a new experimental medication that's being tested in the area.

ENSEMBLE MEMBER 3: And if that wasn't bizarre enough, there have been reports of people spontaneously combusting in some parts of the world. It's as if their bodies are suddenly bursting into flames for no apparent reason.

ENSEMBLE MEMBER 4: There have been reports of people spontaneously combusting for centuries, but the phenomenon is extremely rare and its causes are not yet fully understood.

ENSEMBLE MEMBER 1: The scientific explanation for spontaneous combustion is still a matter of debate among experts, and there is no one agreed-upon theory that can fully explain it.

ENSEMBLE MEMBER 2: However, some scientists believe that spontaneous combustion may be caused by a build-up of flammable gases in the body, such as methane or hydrogen, which can be produced by certain medical conditions or lifestyle factors.

ENSEMBLE MEMBER 3: Others suggest that the combustion could be triggered by an external source of heat or ignition, such as a cigarette or an open flame.

ENSEMBLE MEMBER 4: Still, spontaneous combustion may be a result of a rare combination of factors, including high levels of stress, alcohol consumption, and certain medications, which can lead to a chemical reaction that generates enough heat to ignite the body's tissues.

ALL ENSEMBLE MEMBERS: It's important to note that spontaneous combustion remains a highly controversial and debated topic in the scientific community, and there is still much research to be done to fully understand the phenomenon. But we might be out of time.

>   VOICEOVER *joins in.*

ALL ENSEMBLE MEMBERS/VOICEOVER: Breaking news! The news is broken. There is so much news that there is now no more news. Therefore we will begin a retrospective of the events that shaped all of humanity. Starting now. Unfortunately we cannot stay this way forever. The nature of bubbles is that they burst. We live with that inevitability. You can keep your head down and work but the world will creep up next to you too. Water will rush in.

> *The sound of an 'off air' bell rings and the News Reporters turn into customers and begin the breakaway conversations. The* VOICEOVER *lines that follow add to these conversations, overlapping or underscoring. (It is not important that all the following words are heard, they continue into the section beginning 'The Stone Age'.)*

VOICEOVER: The Hadean eon began four thousand, five hundred and forty million years ago and saw the formation of the planet from a fiery, volcanic landscape with no signs of life. The Archean eon, spanning from four thousand to two thousand, five hundred million years ago, witnessed the emergence of the first form of life, prokaryotes, and the existence of early continents and a hazy atmosphere.

The Proterozoic eon, from two thousand, five hundred to five hundred and thirty-eight-point-eight million years ago, marked the emergence of more complex life, including eukaryotes and multicellular organisms. Bacteria began producing oxygen, and the early and late phases of this eon saw 'Snowball Earth' periods. The Phanerozoic eon, starting from five hundred and thirty-eight-point-eight million years ago to the present, saw the emergence of complex life, including vertebrates, and the formation and dissolution of supercontinents. Life gradually expanded to land, and mass extinctions occurred, paving the way for the emergence of modern animals, including humans.

A large group of customers enter. They start lining up and making orders.

There are three tables with the ENSEMBLE MEMBERS *in groups discussing world events.*

A *and* B *are busy and don't talk unless it's about the customers.*

Table 1:

ENSEMBLE MEMBER 1: Did you hear about the ruling in parliament?

ENSEMBLE MEMBER 2: Ugh let's not talk about it.

ENSEMBLE MEMBER 1: How could they ever let something like that through? Not here not where we live

ENSEMBLE MEMBER 2: I guess we just have to be really careful right now.

ENSEMBLE MEMBER 1: I know, I'm always careful. I really don't want to be pregnant.

ENSEMBLE MEMBER 2: You won't. Just relax.

ENSEMBLE MEMBER 1: Sometimes you can be super-careful and still get pregnant. It happened to my brother and his partner.

ENSEMBLE MEMBER 2: How is your brother?

ENSEMBLE MEMBER 1: They are working a 'fifteen six roster' across the state, but yeah I haven't seen them since, well before—
ENSEMBLE MEMBER 2: Oh yeah
ENSEMBLE MEMBER 1: yeah … I think about it all the time
ENSEMBLE MEMBER 2: Sorry … what?
ENSEMBLE MEMBER 1: Being pregnant, giving birth, it's terrifying
ENSEMBLE MEMBER 2: Don't you think you are being a bit dramatic
ENSEMBLE MEMBER 1: No. not at all.

Table 2:

ENSEMBLE MEMBER 3: Anyway that's why I'm not talking to them right now
ENSEMBLE MEMBER 4: I can't believe it. I just can't believe it.
ENSEMBLE MEMBER 3: I know! It's that person they are dating
ENSEMBLE MEMBER 4: Ugh
ENSEMBLE MEMBER 3: They meet at that weird festival, you know the ones where they go
ENSEMBLE MEMBER 4: They told me that was a eco-futurism festival
ENSEMBLE MEMBER 3: They are trying to
ENSEMBLE MEMBER 4: It's been so dry this summer. I was playing footy and when I hit the ground it almost tore my knee open.
ENSEMBLE MEMBER 3: I can't believe you are still playing. You can't afford to get hurt.
ENSEMBLE MEMBER 4: It is the only thing I actually enjoy doing.
ENSEMBLE MEMBER 3: Why does everyone I know want to hang out in dry fields? It's fire season.
ENSEMBLE MEMBER 4: I'm an athlete
ENSEMBLE MEMBER 3: Well don't come crying to me when you need a knee replacement
ENSEMBLE MEMBER 4: I won't. I will go to the eco festival and get healed
ENSEMBLE MEMBER 3: Are you joking?
ENSEMBLE MEMBER 4: Am I joking?

Table 3:

ENSEMBLE MEMBER 5 *is on the phone—the other side of the conversation* (*in brackets*) *cannot be heard.*

ENSEMBLE MEMBER 5: [*on phone*] You can't be serious, one person can't work those kinds of hours without getting seriously messed up. (*'Under the contract you signed it is legal for the business to roster "flexible" hours.'*) I just don't understand how this is legal. (*'It never used to be legal, just in the last few years.'*) So there really is nothing more we can do. (*'We can take it to the Feds but it will cost more money.'*) I don't have any— (*'I know, I know.'*) I had to pay to get my— (*'Can you borrow some?'*) I suppose I can ask— (*'Ask your dad, just ask him.'*) Fine. I will ask him.

> A *and* B *are serving coffees and café food to the customers at the tables, they interrupt with polite 'Here you go', 'Thank you' and 'Anything else?'*

THE BREAKDOWN

A *tries to depressurise the wand but it starts spraying water everywhere. A pipe bursts in the roof and starts pouring into the café (a shower down from the roof).* A *gets a mop and a bucket. They cannot keep up with the amount of water. This takes a long time. Meanwhile the pressure wand is still spraying at them.*

VOICEOVER: Why won't they do their job? Do something, do anything! It's just water. The world is ending, this is going to happen.

> B *is left dealing with the customers and the running of the café. They are falling behind.*

ENSEMBLE MEMBER 4: Excuse me, can I get another coffee?
B: Sure
ENSEMBLE MEMBER 1: Do you sell anything gluten-free?
B: Yes, just these dessert bars
ENSEMBLE MEMBER 1: Oh ... nothing else?
ENSEMBLE MEMBER 5: It's insane this place doesn't have hot food, all I want is a hot meal
B: I'm sorry the kitchen is closed right now
ENSEMBLE MEMBER 2: I will also have another coffee thanks
B: What did you order?
ENSEMBLE MEMBER 2: Just the same

An ENSEMBLE MEMBER *jumps across the table and attacks their scene partner like an animal, the two are fighting like beasts over a resource.*

A customer who wanted hot coffee built a fireplace out of café tables.

Flora starts growing from the walls and rising up from the ground. We hear birds and mating calls from animals. A dinosaur runs across the stage. An ENSEMBLE MEMBER *comes on stage with a gun like an army officer. Another like a surgeon in full scrubs. Another like a plague doctor.*

Two ENSEMBLE MEMBERS *start kissing, they have sex behind the counter. The line between human and animal is blurred.*

VOICEOVER: The Stone Age, the Nomads of Kabaran Culture, the Dreaming, the Neolithic Revolution, the Rise and Fall of Sumer, the Bronze Age, the Aegean and Minoan Civilisations, the Cradle of Civilisation, Norte Chico Civilisation, Ancient Egypt, the Mature Harappan Phase, Iron Age, Ancient Greece, Ancient Rome, Persian Empire, Qin Dynasty, Byzantine Empire, Early, High and Late Middle Ages, Renaissance Humanism, Protestant Reformation, the European Renaissance, the Enlightenment, Qing Dynasty, First Industrial Revolution, Age of Imperialism, Victorian Era, Second Industrial Revolution, Technological Revolution, World War One, Great Depression, the End of the Sublime Ottoman State, World War Two, Contemporary Period, the Pangolin Plague, Britany's Death, World War Three, the Human Bang. / It's all over, it's done, stop fighting it, you're done.

B: It's over, it's done, stop fighting it, you're done. [*To* A] What are you doing?

A: I was fixing the leak

B: No you're not, you're just standing there.

A: I don't know what to do.

B: You have to try! If you just made the tiniest bit of effort you could achieve something. You are lazy. You only think about yourself, at the whim of whatever impulse you have at the moment. It's actually selfish how little you think of others.

Just cheerfully bulging through everything. You are friendly, but you don't actually care about anyone you smile at. You are fake!

You stand there, or sit there, or lean there, or mill around here, or swing here, or pace over there, or follow me around while holding a cloth and wiping nothing! You're impotent—that's what you are! You are so bloody impotent you can't do your job properly. You're so wrapped up in what the world has been that you have no awareness of what is happening right now. You are the definition of impotence you do not have or show the necessary skills to be successful at anything. I'm sick of listening to you and I'm sick of your voice.

Long pause.

A: Incompetent
B: What?
A: You kept calling me impotent ... but I think you meant incompetent.

B is silent.

A: Also I think you may be projecting just a little—
B: Piss off.

Pause.

A: What did I do to make you hate me?
B: I don't hate you. I don't understand—
A: Why do you have to understand everything? I don't understand anything
B: I can't live like that!

ENDING SEQUENCE

It's raining. Water is leaking into the shop front. A *and* B *are both using mops to fend off the water.*

A: When I get really stressed about the Earth and the world and how messed up everything is, I try to think about when the asteroid came down. The impact alone vaporised so much plant life in the Amazon, but that meant that flowering plants were able to take over and that's the reason humans are able to breathe air now. It was all built out of destruction. Evolution knows how to fill an empty space. That makes me feel better. Something. Anything. Filling an empty space.

Like there are these fish at the bottom of the ocean. Bottom feeders. They never see the light of the sun. The theory was that life needed both sun and water to evolve, to grow. But these creatures prove that life can evolve with just H2O.

That means even when the sun explodes and the Earth is plunged into a forever darkness, something can still grow in the darkness of the ocean. Grow and change. So when there are no more humans. No more creatures like me. There can be some kind of life.

Maybe one day I will be a fossil and they could dig up my life, but they won't know from my bones about my personal failures and emotional pitfalls. Like that I never finish anything I start or that I have never learnt a language other than my own. All the time I have wasted. I struggle every day with simply being a person. I just find it all so hard. Even the most basic task. I don't understand why I exist. But I do. And maybe one day, I will be a fossil.

B: I don't want to stop or slow down. There is no point in sitting here—waiting for it to happen, that is making it worse. That is making it hurt—thinking about it hurts. I need my never-ending chain of premeditated motions. I don't care that it's all a distraction or conforming to the capitalist whatever.

I wish I could think like you, think about my fossil and the future of the world but I can't. I care that I didn't achieve everything I set out to and that I wasted my time on meaningless garbage. But if I think about the number of coffees I made in comparison to the days I spent travelling or oceans I swam in or dates I went on or people I hugged. Because truth be told, I don't have anyone left I care about enough to get that kind of hug. There is no time left to change anything so I just want to be ... until I can't.

A *lies down by the fire, weary.*

B *sits down next to* A.

Have I ever told you a story?
A: You haven't
B: I've got a good story, you'd like it
A: Really? Please tell me.

A *closes their eyes and dies during* B*'s story.* B *hears a low rumble of nature and the T-Rex growl. Sounds from the beginning of the* Jurassic Park *movie in the distance. As the monologue progresses,* B *is drowned out by the soundscape, a swelling of sound like the end of a movie. The* ENSEMBLE *all stand silently looking up at where the* VOICEOVER *came from, they bow once and exit.* B *is still talking to* A *but we can't hear them. The credits roll and the lights go up on the audience. The audience leaves while* B *is still talking to* A. B *and* A *don't leave until the credits finish rolling, they don't bow.*

B: It's night-time, the moon is high and the trees are rustling in the wind. A night worker stares towards the sky as the rustling grows wild. They are joined by an army of men, their attention pointed towards the trees. The leaves are displaced, cut through by a large shipping container carried by a forklift, it is carrying a dinosaur. The men in the distance are shouting in English and Spanish while illuminated by floodlights. They approach quickly, hugging their bodies into the shipping container. The container shakes as they step away and one climbs on top to raise the gate. A strong force of energy sends the container flying backwards leaving a gap between the enclosure and the container. The dinosaur pulls the man on top into the container. A montage of yelling, gritted teeth, slipping hands and eyes with dilated pupils. The river, its serene and quiet rippling over a suited man's reflection as he is hauled into the bank by a team in khakis. They greet one another while walking a plank held by others. Steam and smoke are wafting through the air as they climb the uneven terrain arguing over another man's presence. The suited man slips, smacking his briefcase into the mud. He is more careful now. They continue arguing. They are in a mine now, workers move with torches lit on their heads. The suited man clearly doesn't fit in here. They are still arguing. The sound of metal work and grinding takes over and ceases their conversation for a brief moment. They gather and squat near the newly uncovered yellow rock, a sea of headlights. They smile. The yellow stone holds a small fossilised mosquito. The choir sings. A fossil brush sweeps sand off a greying bone. Across the sand more and more bones are uncovered, more hands, more people. A nostril. A circle of people. It is a full dinosaur now. A man walks up a hill, a woman ties a handkerchief around another man's neck. They put their arms around each other, he touches her ass as they walk down the hill …

THE END

The World According to Dinosaurs

by **Belle Hansen**
and **Amelia Newman**

The World According to Dinosaurs was first produced by Frenzy Theatre Co and La Mama on tour at Platform Arts, Geelong on 4 May, 2023, The Engine Room, Bendigo on 17 May, 2023 and La Mama Courthouse on 24 May, 2023, with the following cast:

A: Amelia Newman
B: Belle Hansen
Ensemble: Izzy Patane, Matilda Gibbs, Anna Louey, Chris Patrick Hansen, Michael Cooper, Emily Pearson

Director, Cassandra Gray
Producer, Flick
Sound Designer and Composer, Jack Burmeister
Lighting Designer, Theo Viney
Education Manager, Alex Veljanovski
Stage Manager, Brigette Jennings

PRODUCTION NOTES

Characters
The two main characters are simply called A and B. They were named as such to give future performers more ownership over the work. For this reason, the characters are also referred to with they/them pronouns, however it's encouraged that future actors adapt these pronouns to what's best for them.

A: Early 20's. A is a nerdy but lazy slacker who doesn't value their job very highly. They love nature and planetology documentaries, but are very passive with what they learn. They lack the courage to apply themselves to anything they might really care about. A has an air of jovial apathy, but deeply longs for connection and excitement.

B: Early 20's. B is hard working and has high standards. They have a low simmering anger and frustration at the world, because they have tried, cared and pushed for social change, but ended up working the same job as A. B fluctuates between relating to A's passion and feeling frustrated at A's laziness. B wants to make the world a better place but feels as though they have been stifled at every opportunity.

Setting
The show is set in a cafe, one you could find in any town. It's not very trendy but it's always busy; you can walk into this cafe in Brunswick or Ballarat and be served by a young person trying to get through their shift. There will be functioning coffee service and a busy set design.

That's until the natural world starts to creep in around the characters. Plants rise up from the floor, vines break through the cracks in the ceiling, dirty water pours out of the kitchen sink. By the end of the show this suburban setting has been fully reclaimed by nature and pollution and decays like the earth itself.

Genre and style glossary

When creating the script, we compiled a list of genres we used or were inspired by (not exhaustive). Some are written into the show, some aren't. Anyone workshopping or staging the text could consider putting in more, or changing the ones that are already there, to suit their production style.

Action	Infomercial	Realism
Adventure	Interview	Reality TV
Animated	Kitchen Sink Realism	Rock Opera
Clown	Morning Show	Satire
Comedy	Musical	Sci-Fi
Crime	Mystery	Silent Film
Dance	Parody	Sitcom
Documentary	Physical Theatre	Slapstick
Drama	Picture Book	Sport
Epic Theatre	Powerpoint	Thriller
Fantasy	presentation	Tragicomedy
Farce	Puppet Theatre	Vaudeville
Horror	Radio Presenter	Western

CREATORS' NOTES

Belle Hansen

The World According to Dinosaurs was developed around the idea that every genre, era and debate would have to come into play when trying to talk about the end of the world.

This work is maximalism. It is the bold uses of colour, pattern and the celebration of excess–more is more.

Frenzy Theatre Co's work is developed with large ensembles of physical performers in an on-floor, task-based style of devising. A very similar approach was taken in the writing with Amelia and myself, using stimulus material and challenges to whip up a first draft of the full show in under two weeks. The scene of the coffee machine breakdown was first drafted with Amelia blasting synthesisers while I tried to write and The Late

Late Underresearched Talk Show was based on one google search and no further fact checking.

For me, writing is most enjoyable and fruitful when it isn't a solo practice. I believe some of the best things come from multiple brains bouncing off one another. I treat the creation of each new scene as a game or challenge and try to do a first version as quickly as possible and think about it later. My hope is that this work encourages performers and theatre makers to write in a way that suits them—you don't have to be good at sitting down and typing it out to be a writer.

Amelia Newman

When I was 12, I wanted to be a palaeontologist. I was fascinated by how humans, using the little information we have, are able to piece together the story of the earth.

The inception of this play began in 2020, when the world was in a time of huge social upheaval and I met Belle Hansen. We worked together on a production that was being rehearsed over Zoom. When I wasn't working as an essential worker at a supermarket, I was watching palaeontology documentaries, re-engaging in my childhood obsession. Once Belle and I could interact in person I would regale her with what I had learnt about prehistoric sloths, palaeozoic crabs and much more.

My favourite documentary was Chris Packham's *The Real T-rex* which is about the inaccuracy of the media representation of the T-rex in movies. It blended media analysis, widely believed yet incorrect information, and fossils. When we were writing this show I was thinking about the stories we tell ourselves and what we believe to be true. Often without really knowing if it's true or not. During this period I was working a lot, while attempting to maintain my arts career as the industry struggled to stay afloat.

This show is about how we attempt to connect with one another in the midst of an ongoing global crisis. It's about making friends and telling stories at the end of the world, and finding the joy in it.

CREATORS' ACKNOWLEDGEMENTS

This work was developed with the support of Brunswick Design District, Merri-Bek City Council, Siteworks and Geelong Arts Centre.

Special Thanks go to –

Development Creatives: Courtney Crisfield, Elizabeth Everett, Sarah Hartnell, Millie Levakis-Lucas and Lucy Orr.

Creative Mentors: Katrina Cornwell and Morgan Rose.

The Team at La Mama, especially Liz Jones for programming *The World According to Dinosaurs* at La Mama Courthouse, as part of the La Mama Learning Program and Maureen Hartley for continuous application, editorial and educational support. Also thanks to La Mama's designer Adam Cass.

And finally, Claire Grady, Katie Pollock and the team at Currency Press for all their assistance with the publication of this book.

CEO & Artistic Director – Caitlin Dullard
Marketing and Communications – Georgina Capper
Development & Pathways Manager – Myf Powell
Venue Technical Manager – Hayley Fox
Producer & Front-of-House Manager – Amber Hart
First Nations Producer/ Curator – Glenn Shea
Learning Producer & School Publications Coordinator - Maureen Hartley
Ticketing & FOH Supervisors – Aya Taur & Gemma Horbury
Design & Marketing Admin – Adam Cass
Online Producer – Ruiqi Fu
Curators:
Gemma Horbury (**Musica**); Amanda Anastasi (**Poetica**)
Isabel Knight (**Cabaretica**); Sophia Constantine
(La Mama for **Kids**)
La Mama Elder – Liz Jones
Documentation – Darren Gill

FRONT OF HOUSE STAFF: Amber Hart, Maureen Hartley, Myf Powell, Laurence Strangio, Hayley Fox, Susan Bamford-Caleo, Dennis Coard, Isabel Knight, Dora Abraham, Ruiqi Fu, Sarah Corridon, Nicki Jam, Aya Taur, Andreas Petropoulos, Dani Hayek, Gemma Horbury, Helen Hopkins, Loukia Vassiliades, Lisa Inman, Maddie Nunn, and Jaye Syson.

COMMITTEE OF MANAGEMENT: Richard Watts (Chair), Helen Hopkins (Dep Chair), Ben Grant, (Treasurer) Caitlin Dullard (Secretary), Members: Caroline Lee, David Geoffrey Hall, Kim Ho, Beng Oh, Mark Williams and Liz Jones.

La Mama Theatre is on traditional land of the people of the Kulin Nation. We give our respect to the Elders of these traditional lands, and to all First Nations people, past and present, and future. We acknowledge all events take place on stolen lands and that sovereignty was never ceded.

La Mama is financially assisted by Creative Victoria (Creative Enterprises Program), and the City of Melbourne (Arts and Creative Partnership Program). We are grateful to all our philanthropic partners and donors, advocates, volunteers, audiences, artists and our entire community. Thank you!

La Mama Theatre & Office is at 205 Faraday St,
Carlton VIC 3053
La Mama Courthouse Theatre, 349 Drummond Street,
Carlton VIC 3053

Tel (03) 9347 6948; Office hours Mon–Fri, 11am–4pm.

www.lamama.com.au
Facebook: lamama.theatre
instagram: lamamatheatre

email: info@lamama.com.au
twitter: LaMamaTheatre

Belle Hansen
Writer/Performer

Belle Hansen is a theatre maker, director and performer who has worked with companies across Australia, including Queensland Theatre, Zen Zen Zo Physical Theatre, Theatre Works and Rawcus. She is a graduate of the Victorian College of the Arts with a Bachelor of Fine Arts (Theatre) and is the Artistic Director of Frenzy Theatre Co. She has performed in many notable programs, including at Malthouse Theatre, Rising Festival, La Mama Courthouse, Martyn Myer Arena, and has had her work seen internationally.

Amelia Newman
Writer/Performer

Amelia Newman is a writer, theatre maker and performer born in Naarm/Melboune. Amelia has worked extensively with Riot Stage Youth Theatre and they have had their work presented at La Mama Theatre, Melbourne Fringe Festival, Northcote Town Hall, Arts House and Siteworks. Amelia's debut play *Younger and Smaller* is published with Australian Plays Transform and has been produced by schools across the country.

Cassandra Gray
Director

Cassandra is a theatre maker and director. Working predominantly with young people, Cassandra sees theatre as a way of enacting change in our world. She has taught and trained in Australia and Asia with companies including Frantic Assembly and 2nd City. She led artist workshops for the Melbourne Theatre Company and regularly teaches at St Martins Youth Arts.

Flick
Producer

Flick is an artist and independent producer. Under FLICKFLICKCITY, Flick looks to produce new Australian works that are bold and glittery. In Naarm, they've produced works with Theatre Works, Motley Bauhaus, Midsumma Festival, Melbourne Fringe, and Frenzy Theatre Co. Flick is currently completing a Master of Theatre (Dramaturgy) at the Victorian College of the Arts, is a member of the Green Room Independent Theatre Panel, and a writer in the 2022/23 Theatre Works SheWrites Collective.

Jack Burmeister
Sound designer/ Composer

Jack Burmeister is a composer who is passionate about finding synergy between his work and other forms of media, believing that music should work to heighten the viewer's overall experience. He uses elements of orchestral, acoustic, electronic, and choral textures to create diverse sonic soundscapes to enhance the atmosphere and mood in any given work. Melody is a key musical characteristic that Jack explores; working to build and enhance melodic devices over the duration of a piece.

Theo Viney
Lighting designer

Theo is a lighting designer currently based in Melbourne and a graduate of the Victorian College of the Arts. He is passionate about creating inventive designs that integrate light with all technical and creative elements of a production. When not designing shows he works as a technician across many of Melbourne's iconic venues.

Brigette Jennings
Stage manager

Brigette is an emerging stage manager, artist and theatre maker based in Naarm/Melbourne. Brigette has been performing, working on stage and backstage since 2014, working with groups such as Frenzy Theatre Co, Dirty Pennies Theatre Project, Theatre Works and Red Stitch.

Isabella Patane
Performer

Isabella Patane is a Naarm/Melbourne-based performer who graduated from Showfit in 2016. Since graduating, she originated the role of 'Bec' in the sold-out Melbourne Fringe show *Teeth and Tonic* written by Megan Scolyer-Gray. Isabella has worked with Frenzy Theatre Company's production of *Motherlod_^e* and is thrilled to be back for *The World According to Dinosaurs*.

Matilda Gibbs
Performer

Anna Louey
Performer

Matilda is a British-Australian theatre maker and performer, originally from Chesham, England. As an instinctual creator, she feels at home interrogating characters through physical and emotional specificity over stereotype. Her most recent theatre credits include *Motherlod_^e* at Theatre Works and *SLUTNIK™* at Melbourne Fringe Festival and Adelaide Fringe Festival.

Anna Louey is an actor and theatre maker from Naarm/Melbourne. She thrives when collaborating with others to create thought-provoking and impactful works. Anna has worked with Frenzy Theatre Co since 2022 on *Motherlod_^e* and *Piper*. She is also a member of the critically acclaimed theatre company Bloomshed, who are known for their highly comedic and political theatre, working on *Paradise Lost* and *Animal Farm*.

Chris Patrick Hansen
Performer

Michael Cooper
Performer

Chris Patrick Hansen is an actor and theatre maker working across Queensland and Victoria. Originally from Brisbane, Chris has trained and performed at some of Queensland's best institutions such as Queensland Theatre, QACI and The Factory Acting Studio. Chris completed his Bachelor in Fine Arts (Theatre) at the Victorian College of the Arts in 2022.

Michael Cooper is a First Nations actor originally from Canberra, now currently based in Naarm/Melbourne. In 2022 he graduated from the Victorian College of the Arts with a BFA in acting. Michael is a committed artist who prides himself on his physical practice and stupid voices.

Emily Pearson
Performer

Emily Pearson is an actor, singer and voiceover artist who trained at the Victorian College of the Arts in a Bachelor of Fine Arts (Acting). Prior to this she completed a Diploma of Music Theatre at the Australian Dance Performance Institute. She is thrilled to be making her professional debut.

Standing Ovation for
Australia's Home of Independent Theatre

In 2023, La Mama celebrates 56 years of nurturing new Australian Theatre, fearlessly facilitating independent theatre making.

Built in 1883 for Anthony Reuben Ford, a Carlton printer, the original building in Faraday Street had been used as a workshop, a boot and shoe factory, an electrical engineering workshop and a silk underwear factory before becoming a theatre in 1967. It was established by Betty Burstall and modelled on experimental theatre activities in New York. Jack Hibberd's play *Three Old Friends* was the first play performed in the tiny space. Since that time the crowded intimacy of La Mama has provided welcome opportunities to a host of playwrights, actors, directors, technicians, film-makers, poets and comedians, such as David Williamson, Barry Dickins, John Romeril, Tes Lyssiotis, Lloyd Jones, the Cantrills, Judith Lucy, Richard Frankland, Julia Zemiro, and Cate Blanchett... the list of both new and experienced theatre makers, and those artists who have been nurtured there, is long.

I set La Mama up, as a space for writers and directors to perform in but also it was a space where people came, as audience, to participate in the creative experiment...

—Betty Burstall, 1987

La Mama Theatre—which on various occasions has been called headquarters, the shopfront and the birthplace of Australian Theatre—was classified by the National Trust in 1999.

The two-storey brick building is of State cultural significance because it has been occupied by La Mama Theatre...The building is indelibly associated with the performance arts and is a rare manifestation of an experimental theatre in Australia...
—National Trust Classification Report

Sadly our home in Faraday Street burned down in May 2018 and, while we were in the process of rebuilding, our home was La Mama Courthouse on Drummond Street Carlton.

Happily, like a phoenix rising from the ashes, our rebuilt La Mama Theatre was reopened in December, 2021 with the War-Rak/ Banksia Festival. (For rebuild details see https://lamama.com.au/rebuild-la-mama)

During its 50-plus years, La Mama has presented approximately 2,500 shows, and we now average around 50 primary production seasons annually, as well as developments, seasonal La Mamica events (Musica, Poetica, Cabaretica, Kids' shows), regular touring through our Mobile program, plus our VCE Learning productions, play readings, and many other special events.

Performances take place again in the restored La Mama, and continue at our second performance venue, the refurbished La Mama Courthouse, 349 Drummond Street.

An ever-increasing audience is drawn to La Mama productions, not only from the Carlton and Melbourne University environs, but from far and wide across the country.

La Mama continues to be an open, accessible space, actively breaking down barriers to the Arts through diverse programs, creative initiatives, affordable ticketing, improved accessible amenities and a welcoming ethos, for performers and audience alike, that has developed over the past five decades. La Mama is home to many and open to all.

For details of all productions and events, and bookings visit: www.lamama.com.au

www.currency.com.au

Visit Currency Press' website now to:
- Buy your books online
- Browse through our full list of titles, from plays to screenplays, books on theatre, film and music, and more
- Choose a play for your school or amateur performance group by cast size and gender
- Obtain information about performance rights
- Find out about theatre productions and other performing arts news across Australia
- For students, read our study guides
- For teachers, access syllabus and other relevant information
- Sign up for our email newsletter

The performing arts publisher

www.ingramcontent.com/pod-product-compliance
Lightning Source LLC
Chambersburg PA
CBHW050026090426
42734CB00021B/3445